SCOTLAN

Postcard Book

24 Classic Photographs by Colin Baxter

Above: Braemar Highland Gathering, Royal Deeside – The Massed Pipe Bands.
Front cover photograph: Eilean Donan Castle, Loch Duich.
Back cover photograph: Lochnagar & Balmoral Castle, Royal Deeside.

LOMOND BOOKS
EDINBURGH • SCOTLAND

SCOTLAND

Two things differentiate Scotland from all other nations of Western Europe – the diversity of its landscape in such a compact and fragmented landmass and the clarity of the light.

When you add to these a quicksilver climate which thrusts fast changes of oceanic weather among islands, mountains, moors, forests, coastal plains and lowland straths, scattering showers and shadows and rainbows across the faces and profiles of ancient rocks, you then have all the ingredients of a natural magic which turns heads and stirs hearts.

The landscape has as many characters as moods. In the Border country, from Galloway in the west to the Berwickshire coast in the east, the hills are blunt and green, and cut by long valleys and great rivers.

At the waist of Scotland, the lowlands of Forth and Clyde are punctuated by a necklace of volcanic 'plugs' – huge isolated rocks which not even the glaciers of the last Ice Age could overwhelm. People have often fortified them, as at Edinburgh, Stirling and Dunbarton. Others have waded out to sea like the Bass Rock and Ailsa Craig.

Highland Scotland is the single mountain realm by which much of the rest of the world remembers us. Yet the Highlands contain great variety. From the Arctic-like plateaux of the Cairngorms to the pinnacled ridges of the Skye Cuillin, from moody Glencoe to the individualist mountains of the north-west like Suilven and Stac Pollaidh, the spectacle is kaleidoscopic.

The charms of island Scotland are no less myriad, from wooded and mountainous Mull to low-slung Coll and Tiree, from palm-treed Gigha to the bare-back rocks and moors of the Western Isles and the ocean outpost of St Kilda. Orkney and Shetland are yet another world, island groups that hark back to their Nordic past in both language and landscape.

Human history has imprinted local architecture on all these, and at its best it enriches them. These postcards are a tantalising taste of Scotland's possibilities to urge your travels, or assist your memories.

First published in Great Britain in 2000 by Lomond Books, 36 West Shore Road, Granton, Edinburgh EH5 1QD Reprinted 2002, 2003, 2004
Photographs Copyright © Colin Baxter 2000   Text Copyright © Colin Baxter Photography Ltd 2000   Text by Jim Crumley
ISBN 1 84204 018 9   Printed in China

Loch Lomond from the air.
Photograph © Colin Baxter.

SCOTLAND

Buachaille Etive Mór, Glencoe.
Photograph © Colin Baxter.

LOMOND BOOKS

SCOTLAND

Iona and the Ross of Mull.
Photograph © Colin Baxter.

LOMOND BOOKS

SCOTLAND

The National Wallace Monument,
Abbey Craig, Stirling.
Photograph © Colin Baxter.

SCOTLAND

The Forth Bridge at dusk.
Photograph © Colin Baxter.

LOMOND BOOKS

SCOTLAND

Pittenweem from the air, Fife.
Photograph © Colin Baxter.

LOMOND BOOKS

SCOTLAND

Loch Creran and Beinn Sgulaird,
Argyll.
Photograph © Colin Baxter.

LOMOND BOOKS

SCOTLAND

Glamis Castle, Angus.
Photograph © Colin Baxter.

LOMOND BOOKS

SCOTLAND

The Cuillin Hills and Loch Dùghaill,
Isle of Skye.

LOMOND BOOKS

SCOTLAND

Kelvingrove Art Gallery & Museum
at dusk, Glasgow.
Photograph © Colin Baxter.

LOMOND BOOKS

S COTLAND

Calanais Standing Stones, Lewis.
Photograph © Colin Baxter.

LOMOND BOOKS

SCOTLAND

Castle Stalker, Appin, Argyll.
Photograph © Colin Baxter.

LOMOND BOOKS

SCOTLAND

Suilven, Sutherland.
Photograph © Colin Baxter.

LOMOND BOOKS

SCOTLAND

Highland Cow.
Photograph © Colin Baxter.

LOMOND BOOKS

SCOTLAND

Stirling Castle.
Photograph © Colin Baxter.

LOMOND BOOKS

S COTLAND

Charles Rennie Mackintosh design
detail from a bookcase now in
Glasgow School of Art.
Photograph © Colin Baxter.

LOMOND BOOKS

SCOTLAND

Eilean Donan Castle, Loch Duich.
Photograph © Colin Baxter.

SCOTLAND

Loch an Eilein, Rothiemurchus and
the Cairngorm Mountains.
Photograph © Colin Baxter.

S COTLAND

Urquhart Castle and Loch Ness.
Photograph © Colin Baxter.

LOMOND BOOKS

SCOTLAND

Glen Barrisdale, Knoydart & Loch Hourn, West Highlands.

Photograph © Colin Baxter.

LOMOND BOOKS

SCOTLAND

Loch Achray, Trossachs.
Photograph © Colin Baxter.

LOMOND BOOKS

SCOTLAND

Point of Sleat, Isle of Skye
– looking towards Eigg & Rum.
Photograph © Colin Baxter.

LOMOND BOOKS

SCOTLAND